BENEATH THE PINES OF KEDDIE

Cabin 28, a Missing Girl, and the Case That Wouldn't Stay Quiet

Linda Davidson

For Sue, John, Tina, and Dana— may memory outlast the silence.

"The truth is rarely pure and never simple."

—OSCAR WILDE

PREFACE

Small towns carry long memories. When a crime strikes such a place, it does not disappear into statistics; it settles into the grain of doors and the hush of evening. The Keddie murders did not only shock a mountain community—they reshaped how a generation thinks about unsolved crimes, forensic gaps, and the steep climb toward justice.

This book follows the facts with care and the people with respect. It acknowledges what we don't yet know, why certain leads failed, and how time both erodes and reveals. If new information emerges—as it often does in cold cases—may it be met with clear eyes and open records.

Content Note

This book includes discussion of homicide and violence involving minors. Reader discretion is advised.

Author's Note on Method & Ethics

I wrote this book with two priorities: accuracy and dignity. Source materials include sheriff's reports, court filings, historical newspapers, FOIA releases, contemporary interviews, and expert analyses. When sources conflicted, I indicate it in the narrative or notes. Where private individuals were not central to the public record, identifying details have been altered. The aim is remembrance, not sensationalism.

A Note on the Case Timeline

A condensed timeline (1980–1984, with subsequent developments) appears before Chapter 1 to ground readers in the sequence of events. A detailed timeline and document notes appear at the back of the book.

DRAMATIS PERSONAE (NON-SPOILER OVERVIEW)

- **Glenna "Sue" Sharp** — Mother at the center of the case.
- **John Sharp** — Sue's son.
- **Tina Sharp** — Sue's daughter.
- **Sheila, Rick, Greg** — Surviving Sharp children referenced in the record.
- **Dana Wingate** — John's friend.
- **First Responders & Investigators** — Plumas County personnel referenced by role/title where appropriate.
- **Key Community Witnesses** — Neighbors and local contacts appearing in the public record.

(Titles and roles reflect the historical period covered.)

ILLUSTRATIONS

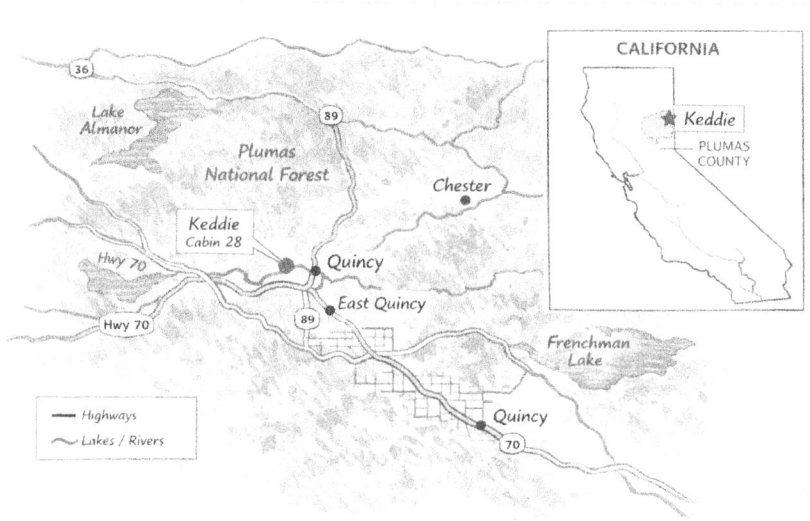

Map of Keddie, California (Regional Context)

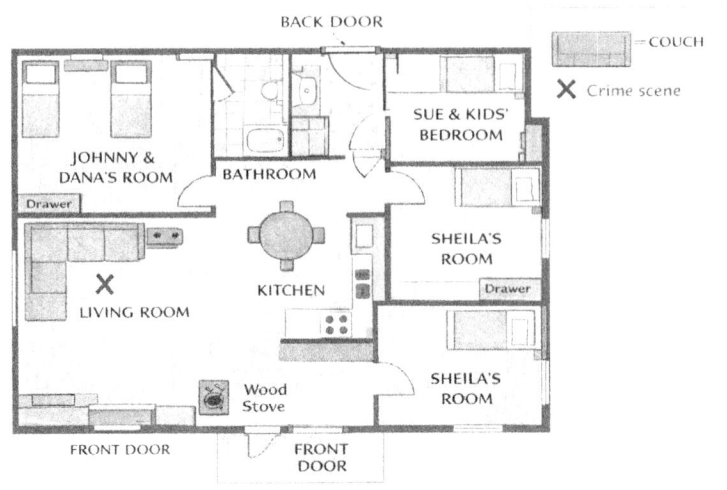

Floor plan of Cabin 28 (schematic representation; not to scale)

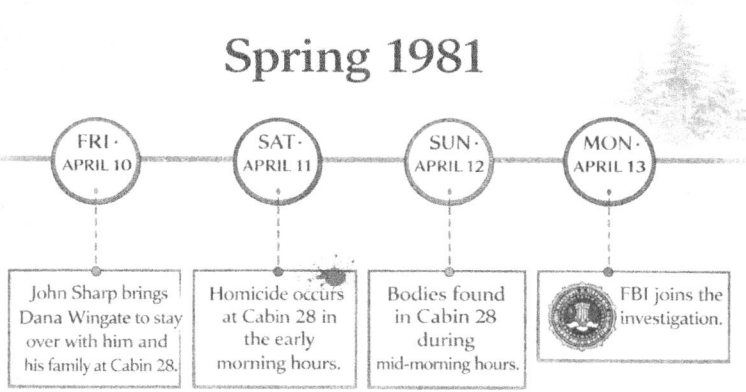

Spring 1981

FRI · APRIL 10	SAT · APRIL 11	SUN · APRIL 12	MON · APRIL 13
John Sharp brings Dana Wingate to stay over with him and his family at Cabin 28.	Homicide occurs at Cabin 28 in the early morning hours.	Bodies found in Cabin 28 during mid-morning hours.	FBI joins the investigation.

Timeline Graphic: Spring 1981

PROLOGUE

— *The Cabin in the Pines*

The Sierra Nevada mountains are beautiful in the way that only isolation can be — tall pines leaning toward a sky the color of faded denim, creeks whispering through the forest, and the sound of your own breath filling the space between. In 1981, the tiny town of Keddie, California, sat quietly in that wilderness, a forgotten pocket of cabins and gravel roads, tucked between the ridges like a secret meant to stay hidden.

At first glance, Keddie was peaceful. Modest wooden cabins lined the hillside, most of them old railroad housing, relics from the time when the Western Pacific Railroad carved through Plumas County. But to those who lived there, it was a place of hardship as much as it was refuge — a place people came to start over, or to disappear.

Cabin 28 was one of the better-kept rentals, a two-story, pale-green structure near the edge of the forest. Inside, it was cramped but homey, filled with secondhand furniture and the laughter of children. The Sharp family had lived there for less than a year — Glenna "Sue" Sharp, a thirty-six-year-old single mother, and her five children: John, Sheila, Tina, Rick, and Greg. Sue had moved her family to Keddie to escape a troubled marriage and build a life she could call her own. It was supposed to be a fresh start.

But on the morning of **April 12, 1981**, that cabin became something else entirely.

Just after sunrise, sixteen-year-old **Sheila Sharp** stepped off the dirt road that led to Cabin 28. She had spent the night at a neighbor's house and was returning home, expecting to find her mother in the kitchen or her brothers still asleep. Instead, she was greeted by a silence so heavy it pressed against her chest.

When she opened the door, she froze.

The scene inside would scar her memory forever.

Three bodies lay in the living room — her mother, **Sue**, her brother **John**, and his friend **Dana Wingate**. They were bound with electrical cords and medical tape, brutally beaten and stabbed. Blood had pooled and smeared across the floor, the walls, and even the ceiling. Chairs were overturned, a knife bent at the handle lay near the door, and a hammer rested among the wreckage.

The youngest children — **Rick, Greg, and Justin**, a friend who had stayed the night — were found alive, asleep in a back bedroom. But **Tina**, the twelve-year-old middle child, was gone.

The quiet town of Keddie awoke that morning to a horror it had never seen before. Deputies from the Plumas County Sheriff's Office arrived quickly, but nothing could prepare them for the brutality waiting inside Cabin 28. What had happened in those shadowed hours between midnight and dawn would baffle investigators for decades.

Neighbors gathered outside, whispering, crying, covering their mouths in disbelief. Keddie had always been small, its residents close enough to know each other's habits and histories. But now, suspicion spread like wildfire. Everyone looked at everyone else with new, fearful eyes. Someone among them had done this.

The cabin itself sat eerily still, as if the trees surrounding it had drawn in a collective breath and never exhaled. Crime scene tape fluttered in the wind like a warning, a fragile barrier between the living and the nightmare that had unfolded within.

In the hours and days that followed, rumors multiplied faster than facts. There were whispers of jealous lovers, of strangers passing through, of local men with violent tempers and darker pasts. The police promised answers. The town prayed for them. But with every passing week, the case grew colder — and the silence in the pines grew heavier.

Years later, those who ventured to the site of Cabin 28 after it was abandoned said the air there still felt wrong — colder, heavier, charged with something unseen. Even after the cabin was demolished, locals claimed they could still feel it, that invisible residue of unsolved violence clinging to the clearing where it once stood.

The Keddie murders became one of California's most haunting unsolved crimes — not just for the brutality, but for the lingering sense that truth had been buried alongside the victims.

To this day, no one has been convicted.

The pines still whisper in the wind.

And in the heart of Plumas County, where shadows fall long across the forest floor, **Cabin 28 remains silent — but never forgotten.**

CHAPTER 1 A FAMILY IN THE WOODS

When **Glenna "Sue" Sharp** packed up her car in the autumn of 1980, she was not just leaving a marriage. She was leaving behind years of fear, humiliation, and disappointment. With five children and barely a hundred dollars to her name, she pointed her old blue Plymouth toward California, determined to find safety and stability in a world that had given her little of either.

Sue had spent most of her adult life being told what she couldn't do — by her husband, by circumstance, by the long shadow of poverty. She had married **James Sharp**, an Air Force veteran, young and hopeful, believing love could protect her from hardship. But over the years, that love had curdled into control and violence. When she finally walked away, she did it quietly, without ceremony or warning. For the first time in her life, she was free — and utterly alone.

She and her children drove west from Connecticut to California, sleeping in rest stops and budget motels. The kids, exhausted but loyal, never complained. They knew their mother's determination meant survival. Somewhere along that endless drive, Sue promised them a new start — a place where they could laugh without fear, sleep without listening for shouting, and dream without dread.

By late 1980, that promise led them to **Keddie**, a small former railroad town nestled in the Sierra Nevada mountains of northern California. It wasn't much to look at — a scattering of rustic cabins, pine needles blanketing the roads, and the faint hum of trains winding through the canyon. But to Sue, it felt like sanctuary.

The family moved into **Cabin 28**, a weathered, two-story rental with green siding and a creaky wooden porch. The rent was only $170 a month — cheap enough to make survival possible. Inside, there was little furniture, but the home smelled of pine and freedom. Sue's teenage son **John**, the oldest at fifteen, helped her fix broken boards and move in what little they owned. **Sheila**, sixteen, often watched over her younger siblings — **Tina**, twelve, and the youngest boys, **Rick** and **Greg**, ages ten and five.

Life in Keddie was modest, but it was theirs.

A Mother's Quiet Strength

Neighbors described Sue as shy but kind. She wore her hair straight and brown, often tucked behind her ears, and she smiled easily even when she looked tired. She wasn't one for gossip or parties. Most days, she stayed home, sewing clothes for her children, reading library books, or walking the winding paths behind the cabins.

At night, when the children slept, she wrote letters — sometimes to her sister, sometimes to herself — trying to untangle the exhaustion that clung to her heart. She had dreams, though she rarely spoke them aloud. She wanted to take college classes, to earn a nursing degree, to show her children that starting over didn't mean staying stuck.

Her life wasn't glamorous, but it was honest. She took odd jobs, relied on welfare checks, and stretched every dollar like elastic. The Sharp children learned early the value of resourcefulness — how to make dinner out of canned beans and rice, how to share one coat between two siblings, how to keep each other warm in winter when the heater broke.

But despite the hardship, there was laughter in that cabin — loud, pure, unguarded laughter that filled the pine air like music.

The Sharp Children

Each child carried a piece of Sue's spirit.

Sheila, mature beyond her years, was the caretaker — protective, observant, already motherly.

John, quiet but rebellious, wanted to leave small-town life behind and make something of himself.

Tina, bright and sensitive, idolized her mother and dreamed of becoming a dancer or actress.

The younger boys, **Rick** and **Greg**, were bundles of energy, often found climbing trees or building forts near the creek.

They didn't have much, but they had each other — and in a place like Keddie, that was enough.

The neighbors, too, were a strange assortment of survivors. Some were families like the Sharps, scraping by on little; others were drifters, men with inconsistent work and heavy drinking habits. The cabins were close enough to hear voices through thin walls at night, yet far enough apart for secrets to stay buried.

Keddie: The Town Time Forgot

In 1981, Keddie wasn't much more than a handful of cabins surrounded by forest, a place that seemed to exist outside of time. The old **Keddie Resort** had once been a thriving railroad stop, but by the 1980s, it had decayed into a cluster of low-rent housing units managed by the Meeks family. The nearest town, **Quincy**, was several miles away — a small but slightly more developed community where most residents worked, shopped, and socialized.

Life in Keddie moved at the pace of the wind. Kids biked down dirt paths, played near the creek, and came home when the sun dipped below the ridgeline. The Sharp children quickly blended into that rhythm. They made friends with neighborhood kids, including **Justin Smartt**, who often visited their cabin and became especially close to the younger boys.

To the Sharps, it seemed like they had found the quiet life they'd been searching for — a chance to heal, to grow roots.

But beneath Keddie's calm surface, something darker stirred.

There were whispers of domestic fights, drugs, and strange visitors who came and went at odd hours. Some cabins, locals said, weren't as innocent as they looked. It was a place where broken people came to hide — and where past sins could stay unspoken.

Hope and Shadows

In early April 1981, Sue confided to a neighbor that she felt uneasy. She didn't say why, only that she had "a bad feeling lately." She'd been studying part-time and counseling another woman going through a separation — a gesture of empathy that might have drawn unwanted attention. Some reports later suggested she had rejected the advances of a local man, one with a temper and friends in law enforcement.

Whatever it was, Sue brushed it aside, focusing instead on her kids' futures. She kept routines steady — dinners together, curfews enforced, kindness expected. For all her exhaustion, she refused to let bitterness define her home.

On **April 11, 1981**, the day before the murders, the Sharp children went about life as usual. John and his friend **Dana Wingate** spent the afternoon in Quincy. Sheila planned a sleepover with a friend. The younger boys played in the yard until dusk, their laughter echoing through the trees. Sue made dinner, tidied up, and sat at the kitchen table that night — perhaps writing, perhaps thinking.

Outside, the forest was calm. The mountains stood tall, indifferent to human fear.

Within hours, Cabin 28 would be filled with screams that no one heard — and a silence that would last for decades.

CHAPTER 2 THE NIGHT OF APRIL 11, 1981

The evening of **April 11, 1981**, began like any other in the small mountain community of Keddie. The spring air was crisp, carrying the scent of pine and woodsmoke, and the faint hum of crickets rose with the dusk. In the Sharp household, Cabin 28, the day had been ordinary — filled with chores, laughter, and the constant rhythm of life that Sue fought so hard to keep steady.

But as the sun dipped behind the trees and the shadows deepened, the ordinary began to unravel.

An Ordinary Evening

Inside the cabin, Sue prepared dinner while her youngest boys — **Rick** and **Greg** — played in their shared bedroom. **Justin Smartt**, their neighborhood friend and frequent visitor, was spending the night. His mother, **Marilyn Smartt**, lived nearby in Cabin 26 with her husband **Martin "Marty" Smartt**, a former cook at the

Veterans Hospital in Reno. Justin was quiet and polite, a good kid, though sometimes nervous around adults. Sue welcomed him like one of her own.

That evening, **Sheila**, Sue's sixteen-year-old daughter, was preparing to sleep over at the Seabolt family's cabin next door. It was just a few yards away, separated by trees and a patch of uneven ground. Sheila hugged her mother goodnight, said she'd see everyone in the morning, and stepped out into the cool mountain air — unaware that it would be the last time she would ever see her mother alive.

Inside Cabin 28, Sue's other daughter, **Tina**, had joined her brothers and Justin for a few minutes before heading to a friend's nearby home. She spent the early part of the evening at the Seabolt cabin as well but returned home later that night, sometime around 9:30 or 10:00 p.m.

In the living room, **John Sharp**, fifteen, and his best friend **Dana Wingate**, seventeen, came and went, teenage energy filling the space. They had spent the day hitchhiking into Quincy, hanging out with friends, and were now back in Keddie, laughing and teasing each other like boys who believed they still had time.

The small home was full but peaceful — a family gathered under one roof, unaware that death was already on its way.

A Town Settles In

By ten o'clock, Keddie was mostly asleep. The town had no nightlife, no bars or neon lights, only the hum of the forest and the occasional bark of a dog. The cabins were dark, windows glowing faintly from television sets or bedside lamps.

At the Seabolts', Sheila lay awake talking quietly with her friend. At Cabin 26, just a short walk away, Marilyn Smartt sat alone. Her husband Marty was reportedly out drinking with a friend — a man named **"Bo" Boubede**, an older ex-con who had recently come to stay with them. Bo was said to have ties to organized crime and had served time in Chicago. Locals didn't know much about him, only that he dressed sharply and carried himself like a man used to being feared.

That night, Bo and Marty supposedly returned to the Smartt home late. Marilyn would later recall an uneasiness she couldn't explain. She went to bed early, leaving the two men awake in the living room.

Across the way, the Sharps' lights were still on.

Somewhere Between Midnight and Dawn

No one can say exactly when the peace of Cabin 28 shattered. Somewhere between midnight and 2:00 a.m., the Sharp home became a chamber of horror.

There were no signs of forced entry — only the faint impression that the door had been opened willingly, perhaps to someone familiar. The attack, when it came, was swift and frenzied.

In the living room, Sue, John, and Dana faced a level of violence that suggested both rage and control. They were bound with medical tape and extension cords. John and Dana were beaten repeatedly with a hammer; Dana was strangled with a length of electrical wire. Sue, still wearing her robe, had been bludgeoned and stabbed, her wrists bound tightly.

The killers — believed to be more than one — had methodically destroyed the family. Nothing valuable was taken. No sexual assault was confirmed. Whatever happened that night, it wasn't a robbery. It was personal.

In the small bedroom down the hall, the younger boys — Rick, Greg, and Justin — slept through the chaos, untouched. Some investigators believe they may have seen or heard something, but fear or confusion kept them still.

And then there was **Tina**.

By morning, she was gone.

The Witness Who Slept

In later years, Justin Smartt would tell conflicting stories about that night. At first, he claimed to have slept through everything. Then, during hypnosis sessions with investigators, he described dreams — vivid, disturbing scenes of men attacking Sue and the others, and of Tina being taken out the back door.

In his recollection, one of the men was wearing glasses. Another had a mustache. The dream blurred into reality, leaving investigators unsure what to believe. Was it imagination? A repressed memory? Or something else entirely — a child's fragmented attempt to recall a trauma too terrible to face?

Whatever Justin saw, it would haunt him for the rest of his life.

The Stillness Before Discovery

By dawn, the forest outside Cabin 28 was calm again. The birds began their morning calls, the sun filtering through the pines, indifferent to what lay beyond the thin walls of the Sharp home.

Inside, the air was heavy, the silence absolute. Three lives had been taken. One had vanished. And three young boys, still asleep in the back room, breathed on — blissfully unaware of the devastation just beyond their door.

At 7:45 a.m., as the mist lifted off the mountain road, **Sheila Sharp** returned home from her sleepover. She walked up the familiar steps, opened the front door, and stepped into a world that would never be the same.

She screamed.

Her voice echoed across the cabins, piercing the quiet morning like a siren. Neighbors rushed from their doors, running toward the sound.

Inside, the scene was beyond comprehension — blood spattered on walls, overturned furniture, the bodies of her mother, her brother, and his friend bound and broken on the floor.

And where Tina should have been — there was only emptiness.

The Keddie murders had begun their long shadow across time.

CHAPTER 3 THE SCENE OF HORROR

The morning of **April 12, 1981**, dawned cold and deceptively still. The first beams of sunlight filtered through the towering pines, painting long, slanted shadows across the cabins in the small, secluded community of Keddie. It was the kind of quiet morning that should have begun with the sound of breakfast dishes clinking and children running outside to play.

Instead, a scream shattered the peace.

A Daughter's Discovery

Sixteen-year-old **Sheila Sharp** had no reason to expect anything unusual that morning. She had spent the night at the Seabolt family's cabin, less than fifty feet away, laughing with her friend and talking about teenage things — music, school, boys. When she left for home shortly after 7:45 a.m., she carried only a small overnight bag and a light heart.

As she approached **Cabin 28**, the door stood closed, and all seemed quiet. The curtains hung still. Birds chattered overhead. She turned the knob and stepped inside.

Then she froze.

Before her eyes, the living room unfolded like a nightmare painted in red. Three bodies lay sprawled across the floor. Her mother, **Sue Sharp**, lay closest to the couch, partially covered with a blanket, her wrists and ankles bound with tape and electrical cords. Near her, **John Sharp**, just fifteen, and his best friend **Dana Wingate** were tangled together — beaten, stabbed, and bound in the same way.

Blood was everywhere.

It streaked the walls, soaked into the carpet, and sprayed across the furniture in wide, violent arcs. The lamp had been knocked over, and the coffee table shattered into splinters. One of the knives lay bent at the handle.

For a moment, Sheila could not move. Her mind refused to understand what her eyes were seeing. Then, as reality slammed into her, she screamed — a raw, piercing sound that echoed through the quiet mountain air.

The First Responders

The Seabolts heard her cries and came running. When they saw what was inside Cabin 28, they turned pale and staggered back. One of them ran to call law enforcement from a nearby phone.

Meanwhile, Sheila's thoughts turned to her siblings. **Tina**, **Rick**, and **Greg** — where were they? Were they among the bodies? Were they alive?

The adults outside were too frightened to reenter the cabin, so Sheila, trembling and determined, climbed through a bedroom window to reach her younger brothers. Inside the small room, the three boys lay in their sleeping bags, untouched, their faces peaceful.

They had slept through the entire massacre.

Sheila gently guided them out through the same window, away

from the sight that waited in the living room. She whispered to them not to look, not to ask, just to go.

When Sheriff's deputies from **Plumas County** arrived minutes later, they found chaos. Neighbors huddled outside, weeping. Children clung to each other, whispering about screams no one had actually heard. The entire town seemed to hold its breath as officers crossed the threshold into the cabin.

Nothing could have prepared them for what they saw.

A Scene of Unspeakable Violence

In all their years on duty, the deputies had never witnessed anything like the carnage that filled Cabin 28. The killings had been brutal and deliberate.

Sue's injuries were extensive — she had been bludgeoned with a hammer and stabbed multiple times in the chest and neck. A piece of medical tape covered her mouth, as if to silence her screams. Her hands were bound tightly, defensive wounds visible across her arms.

John's throat had been cut, and his head had suffered severe blunt-force trauma. Dana's death appeared to be the result of strangulation and head injuries. Both boys were tied with electrical cords, their bindings connecting them to each other in a grim tableau.

The living room showed signs of struggle. Chairs were overturned, the television toppled, and a curtain rod bent out of shape. A hammer lay near Sue's body, its handle slick with blood. Another knife, its blade bent from force, rested near the couch.

Yet oddly, there was no sign of forced entry. The door was unlocked. Nothing appeared stolen. And the youngest children had been spared.

It was clear this was no random act of violence. Whoever had done this had spent time inside the cabin — enough to stage the scene, wipe certain surfaces, and possibly take something, or someone, with them.

That "someone" was **Tina Sharp**.

Her bed was empty. Her shoes were gone. Her jacket, too. But there was no blood in her room, no sign of a struggle. It was as though she had simply vanished into the night.

The Investigation Begins — and Fails

The initial response from the **Plumas County Sheriff's Office** was disorganized and careless, a failure that would haunt the case for decades. Deputies failed to immediately cordon off the crime scene, allowing neighbors, reporters, and even curious onlookers to wander close enough to contaminate evidence.

Inside, footprints overlapped. Objects were moved. Cigarette butts and fingerprints were collected but never properly cataloged. The small-town department was overwhelmed — they had never handled a multiple homicide before, and their resources were limited.

Sheriff **Doug Thomas** took charge, promising a thorough investigation. But almost from the beginning, mistakes piled up. Leads were followed haphazardly. Evidence disappeared. Interviews were rushed or never conducted.

Within hours, the cabin became a maze of confusion.

Outside, television crews began arriving, their cameras capturing the haunting image of the pale-green house surrounded by crime scene tape. The nation would soon know its name: **Cabin 28**.

A Town in Fear

As word spread, the small community of Keddie descended into panic. Doors that had never been locked before now bolted shut. Children were kept inside. Neighbors eyed one another with suspicion. The sense of safety that had once defined the town evaporated overnight.

At the grocery store in nearby Quincy, whispers filled the aisles. Some said it was the work of a drifter. Others believed it was personal — revenge, jealousy, maybe something darker.

But those who knew Sue Sharp struggled to imagine who could hate her enough to destroy her family. She was kind, private, gentle. She didn't drink, didn't party, didn't cause trouble. She was the kind of woman who lent sugar to her neighbors and gave advice to anyone in pain.

And yet, someone had stood in her living room and slaughtered her without mercy.

The Missing Piece

As investigators searched for Tina, helicopters combed the forest while deputies scoured nearby trails and creeks. Nothing. It was as if the girl had vanished into the woods themselves.

For months, her disappearance haunted the investigation. Who had taken her — and why spare her brothers? Was she a witness? A target? Or both?

The unanswered questions stacked higher than the evidence. And in a case already slipping through the cracks of poor procedure and local fear, every passing day made the truth harder to find.

Cabin 28 was eventually boarded up, left as it had been — bloodstained walls, broken furniture, and an aura of despair that clung to it long after the police left.

Locals said you could still smell the iron tang of blood inside, even years later. Others claimed that at night, you could hear faint echoes — the sound of a door creaking open, or a soft voice calling a name that never received an answer.

The Sharp family's refuge had become a tomb.

And in that silence, the story of Keddie was only beginning.

CHAPTER 4 SUSPECTS AND SECRETS

In the days that followed the Keddie murders, fear gripped the mountains like frost. The cabin sat dark, sealed with police tape, its windows boarded and its silence unnerving. For a small, close-knit community that had once left doors unlocked, everything changed overnight. People whispered names, replayed rumors, and wondered which of their neighbors might be capable of something so cruel.

And in those whispers, two names surfaced again and again.

Martin "Marty" Smartt and **John "Bo" Boubede**.

The Man Next Door

Martin Smartt lived just a few cabins away from the Sharps — in **Cabin 26**, to be exact. On the outside, he looked like a hardworking man: a former cook who had served in the military, a husband and father trying to make ends meet. But beneath that image, there was tension — a temper that flashed quick, and a marriage unraveling under the weight of secrets.

His wife, **Marilyn**, was a friend of Sue Sharp's. The two women shared coffee, stories, and quiet conversations about raising children and enduring hardship. Sue had become something of a confidante to Marilyn, who often confided in her about Marty's temper. According to some reports, Sue encouraged her to leave him — advice that may have angered Marty deeply.

Then there was **"Bo" Boubede**, an older man with slicked-back hair, sharp suits, and a past no one fully understood. He was a friend of Marty's from his time working in Reno. Bo had reportedly served in the military and done prison time. Some whispered that he was connected to organized crime, maybe even a government informant. Others said he was just a drifter who had charmed his way into Keddie.

Together, Marty and Bo made an odd pair — inseparable drinking buddies, unpredictable when fueled by alcohol and resentment.

And the night of **April 11, 1981**, both men were in Keddie.

The Night They Can't Explain

According to statements later given to investigators, Marty and Bo spent that evening at the **Keddie Bar** before returning home sometime after midnight. Marilyn recalled hearing them come in — drunk, agitated, whispering harshly. When she woke the next morning, Marty was gone again.

She later claimed that her husband burned something in the wood stove that morning — papers, maybe clothes — and that his behavior was strangely distant.

At first, she dismissed the unease as paranoia, but when news of the Sharp murders broke, she felt sick. Her husband's cabin was just a short walk from Cabin 28. The timing, the rage she had seen before in him, the silence that followed — it all began to connect in her mind.

Marty, when questioned by police, gave vague answers. He claimed to have no idea what happened, and he cooperated — to a point. Bo, too, denied any involvement.

But from the start, their alibis didn't hold up.

The two men claimed they had been asleep or watching television during the estimated time of the murders. Yet others said they were seen leaving the bar late, angry and drunk. One bartender recalled an argument between Marty and another patron about his wife — and about Sue Sharp.

Investigators noted inconsistencies but never pressed too hard. For reasons that still baffle true crime researchers today, both men were treated gently.

The Boy Who Remembered Too Much

The most chilling lead came not from adults but from a child — **Justin Smartt**, Marty's twelve-year-old stepson, who had been sleeping in the Sharp cabin that night.

At first, Justin told investigators he had slept through everything. But his demeanor was tense, his eyes distant, and his drawings — made at the request of detectives — were disturbing. He drew scenes of violence that mirrored the crime: people bound, attacked, and one small figure being led away from the house.

Later, during a **hypnosis session** conducted by a police therapist, Justin described what he called a "dream." In it, he saw two men in the Sharp cabin — one with long hair and glasses, the other with a mustache. He said they argued with Sue, then began attacking her and the boys. He remembered one of them taking **Tina** out the back door, into the dark.

The hypnosis session, though controversial, revealed details that unnerved investigators — especially when Justin identified the men in sketches resembling his stepfather and Bo.

Still, the Plumas County Sheriff's Office hesitated. Sheriff **Doug Thomas** and Investigator **Mike Gamberg** were at odds; Gamberg believed the case pointed directly to Marty, while Thomas seemed to shield him from deeper scrutiny. Years later, Gamberg would openly state that law enforcement "protected" certain individuals during the investigation.

At the time, however, Marty was questioned and released.

Bo quietly left town soon after.

The Letter

Months later, as the investigation floundered and public frustration grew, an envelope arrived at the **Plumas County Sheriff's Office**. Inside was a letter, handwritten by Marty Smartt, addressed to his wife Marilyn.

It read:

"I've paid the price of your love and now that I've bought it with four lives, you tell me we are through.

Great. What else do you want?"

The letter was signed, simply, "Love, Marty."

When investigators found it, they reportedly dismissed it as "emotional nonsense" — a bitter letter from a man in a failing marriage. But to anyone familiar with the case, its implications were chilling. Four lives. The number matched perfectly: Sue, John, Dana, and Tina.

Years later, when the case was reopened, new detectives would call the letter a near-confession.

But in 1981, it was brushed aside.

Protected Shadows

The deeper investigators looked, the stranger things became. Evidence had gone missing. Statements were altered. Certain names were quietly erased from reports.

Sheriff Thomas, it turned out, was close friends with Marty Smartt. When questioned years later about his handling of the case, he insisted that friendship had not influenced his actions — but those who worked under him weren't convinced.

Within weeks of the murders, both Marty and Bo left Keddie. Bo returned to Chicago, disappearing from California entirely. Marty eventually settled elsewhere in the state, remarrying and living a quiet life. He would die in 2000, never charged, never confessing.

Meanwhile, the Sharp family's pain deepened. **Tina** was still missing, her disappearance a wound that refused to heal. Sheila and her surviving brothers were placed in foster care, their lives fractured beyond repair.

The case grew cold — not because the trail had gone dry, but because it had been buried.

And beneath that silence, the truth festered.

CHAPTER 5 TINA'S VANISHING

The forest around Keddie was vast — a patchwork of pine and shadow stretching for miles across Plumas County. In the days following the massacre inside Cabin 28, that forest swallowed a secret no one could find. A twelve-year-old girl was missing. Her name was **Tina Sharp**.

She had vanished sometime between midnight and dawn, leaving behind a house soaked in violence and a town paralyzed by fear. The question that haunted investigators from the moment they saw her empty bed was simple: *Did she run… or was she taken?*

The Vanished Child

Tina was the third of Sue Sharp's five children — quiet, sweet-natured, and artistic. She loved drawing pictures of horses and listening to pop music on her small radio. Those who knew her remembered the way she trailed after her older siblings, eager to belong. At school, she was shy but well-liked. Her teachers said she had a gentle heart, the kind of child who shared lunches and defended smaller kids from teasing.

When police combed through Cabin 28 that April morning, there was no trace of her — no footprints leading away from the cabin, no blood, no sign of a struggle in her room. Her shoes and jacket were gone, suggesting she might have been awake when the attack began. But whether she left willingly or was forced into the night remained unknown.

For a mother who had already suffered so much, Sue's absence would soon be joined by her daughter's silence. Tina had been erased from the scene as completely as if the forest itself had swallowed her whole.

The Search That Found Nothing

Within hours of the discovery, **search parties** fanned out through the mountains. Deputies, volunteers, and even dogs scoured the area around Keddie and the nearby Feather River. Helicopters circled overhead, their spotlights slicing through the trees at night.

Every noise in the woods became a possibility. Every broken branch, a clue.

But the terrain worked against them. Steep canyons, thick undergrowth, and miles of wilderness made any thorough search almost impossible. The weather turned cold, and the sense of hope that fueled the first days quickly began to fade.

At the time, missing-person investigations in small rural departments were limited. There were no national databases, no digital coordination. Leads came through phone calls, tips, and rumors — and rumors in Keddie were endless. Some said Tina had run away, traumatized by what she'd seen. Others whispered that she had been taken by the killers to keep her silent.

Her school friends wept in class; the teachers held small vigils. For weeks, flyers with her photograph — a brown-haired girl with soft eyes and a hesitant smile — hung on telephone poles and gas-station walls across Plumas County.

But as spring turned to summer, no one found a trace of her.

The Psychic Trail

Desperate for answers, law enforcement — and even the Sharp family — turned to unconventional help. Several **psychics** claimed to know where Tina was. One described "a body near water and trees." Another mentioned an old mining area. Tips poured in from across California, none leading anywhere solid.

The media seized on the story, painting Keddie as a place haunted by both violence and mystery. Headlines called the case "The Cabin Murders" and "The Vanishing Girl of Plumas County." Reporters arrived, only to find a wall of silence. Locals stopped talking to outsiders, afraid or distrustful.

Behind closed doors, investigators continued to circle around the same suspects — Martin Smartt and "Bo" Boubede — but without Tina, there was no way to prove what had happened. She was the missing witness, the key to understanding that night.

And somewhere, out there in the endless woods, she was still gone.

Three Years of Silence

Time is cruel in missing-person cases. After the first few weeks, even the most determined searches slow. After months, they stop.

By 1982, the Sharp family had moved away from Keddie. The cabin remained abandoned, its windows boarded and its past sealed within. Residents tried to forget, but the name Tina Sharp lingered like an echo.

Sheriff's deputies occasionally revisited tips, but no evidence surfaced — no clothing, no bones, no answers. Some theorized that animals had carried her remains deep into the wilderness. Others believed she had been buried intentionally.

The file on her case grew thinner as the years passed, the pages yellowing under dust. Then, in **April 1984**, fate finally shifted.

The Discovery at Feather Falls

A man collecting bottles in the **Feather Falls** area — roughly a hundred miles from Keddie — stumbled upon something strange. Near an old logging road lay a human skull, partially buried under leaves and soil.

At first, he assumed it was an animal bone. But when he looked closer, the size and shape told a different story. He called the authorities.

Forensic experts from **Butte County** arrived and began excavating the site. Alongside the skull, they found fragments of a jawbone, vertebrae, and pieces of a child's clothing — faded, weather-worn, and long forgotten by time.

Nearby, a child's blanket lay tangled in the brush.

When dental records were compared to those of the missing girl from Keddie, the match was unmistakable. The remains belonged to **Tina Sharp**.

She had been found exactly three years after she disappeared — to the day. April 1984.

The discovery reignited the case, but it also deepened the mystery. How had her body ended up so far from Keddie? Who had taken her there? And why?

The Questions That Wouldn't Die

Forensic analysis in the 1980s could not determine a clear cause of death. The bones showed no obvious trauma, and decomposition had erased any hope of recovering DNA evidence. What investigators could tell was that Tina had died not long after the murders.

Her remains had been moved — perhaps driven into the mountains by her killers in the dark hours after the crime. The area where she was found was remote, accessible only by rough dirt roads. Whoever left her there knew the land well.

When Sheriff's deputies announced the identification, the news reached the surviving Sharp children like a knife reopening an old wound. For Sheila, the sister who had found the bodies, the revelation confirmed what she had feared all along: Tina hadn't run away. She had been taken — and murdered.

The official investigation barely flickered to life before fading again. Leads dried up, suspects had long since vanished, and the sense of unfinished justice settled over Keddie like fog.

Years later, when the case would be reopened, detectives would return to the Feather Falls discovery site with fresh eyes and modern tools, hoping to extract DNA or find overlooked clues. But in 1984, the technology simply didn't exist.

All they had was a name, a handful of bones, and a grief that would never heal.

The Silence After

After Tina's remains were found, the investigation stalled once more, swallowed by bureaucracy and indifference. The official word was that the case was still open — but in practice, it sat cold and forgotten, like the cabin itself.

In the small mountain town of Keddie, people spoke of her in hushed tones. Some believed her spirit lingered in the pines, trying to lead someone to the truth. Others avoided the subject entirely, afraid to stir whatever darkness had once walked among them.

For the Sharp family, there was no closure — only survival. They had lost a mother, a brother, a friend, and now the little girl who might have been the key to it all.

The forest that had swallowed her secret kept it still.

And as the years passed, the legend of the Keddie murders hardened into something darker — a wound time refused to heal, a question that refused to fade.

CHAPTER 6
CORRUPTION AND
COVER-UPS

The murders in Cabin 28 should have shaken California law enforcement to its core. Three people slaughtered, a child vanished, and a crime scene so brutal it was burned into every deputy's memory. Instead, within months of that April morning in 1981, the case was slipping quietly into obscurity—suffocated not by lack of evidence, but by **mistrust, mishandling, and the politics of a small mountain county.**

The Investigation That Never Was

At first, Sheriff **Doug Thomas** promised the community swift justice. He appeared on local radio assuring residents that his department had "strong leads." But behind closed doors, his deputies were lost. Evidence collected from the Sharp home—

blood samples, fingerprints, even a bloody knife—was sent to labs and never returned, or simply vanished into storage boxes with no catalog numbers.

Officers walked through the cabin without gloves. Cigarette butts from onlookers mixed with those of potential suspects. When crime-scene photos were later reviewed, entire sections of the room were missing from documentation.

Even more disturbing, certain names were quietly erased from follow-up reports. **Martin Smartt** and **"Bo" Boubede**, both interviewed early on, were dropped from the suspect list within weeks. No formal polygraph tests were administered. No search warrants were issued for their home or vehicles.

When one deputy questioned the decision, he was told to "leave it alone."

The Sheriff and His Friend

Rumors spread quickly through Quincy—the nearest town with a working police office—that Sheriff Thomas and Marty Smartt were close. They had attended the same veteran's gatherings and occasionally drank together at the local bar.

When journalists asked about the connection, Thomas brushed it off. "Small town," he said. "Everyone knows everyone."

But the optics were damning. Thomas had personally signed off on releasing Marty and Bo after only brief questioning, despite inconsistent alibis and the proximity of their cabin to the crime scene.

Years later, retired deputies would admit that many inside the department believed Thomas had deliberately shielded his friend. One investigator recalled, *"If you mentioned Smartt's name too many times, your report got 'lost.'"*

Evidence Gone, Voices Silenced

By the mid-1980s, the case file was a labyrinth of contradictions. Reports referred to missing photographs, mislabeled fingerprint cards, and tapes that no longer existed. Even the **confession-style letter** Marty had written to his wife—"I've paid the price of your love with four lives"—was dismissed as melodrama and filed away without forensic testing.

When **Tina Sharp's remains** were discovered in 1984, the sheriff's office promised a renewed effort. For a few weeks, investigators dusted off boxes and reopened interviews. But the momentum faded almost instantly. Sheriff Thomas retired soon after, taking with him whatever knowledge he had of the early investigation.

The files were boxed, stacked, and forgotten in the basement of the Plumas County Sheriff's Department—unlabeled, unindexed, gathering dust.

For the Sharp family, every phone call to the department ended the same way: "We're still working on it." They weren't.

The Long Silence

The 1990s passed with only brief flickers of hope. A handful of television specials revived public interest, showing grainy photographs of the cabin and police sketches that looked eerily like Marty Smartt. Each broadcast brought a wave of tips, none pursued seriously.

Inside Keddie, the once-thriving resort community collapsed into decay. Cabins emptied. Roofs caved. Cabin 28 stood like a scar in the trees—boarded, weather-stained, and silent. Locals said they could still feel something there, as if the forest itself refused to forget.

Sheila Sharp, now an adult with children of her own, continued writing letters to law enforcement. She begged them not to let the case die. Sometimes she got polite replies. More often, silence.

A New Generation of Investigators

In the early 2000s, a shift began. Retired Plumas County Sheriff's Investigator **Mike Gamberg**, a man who had been on the force during the original investigation but was kept away from the case, decided to look again.

He had spent decades haunted by what he'd seen—the way evidence had disappeared, how leads were ignored. When he returned to the department in a part-time capacity, he began digging through storage.

What he found stunned him: **a box of forgotten files**, unmarked and dusty, containing photographs, reports, and even items of physical evidence that had never been tested. Among them were blood-stained tape, a hammer matching the murder weapon's description, and an audio cassette with a chilling message left on a tip line in the 1980s.

The anonymous caller's voice was calm, almost rehearsed:

"I was watching the news about the girl found at Feather Falls... I know who killed the Sharp family."

Then the tape ended.

No name. No callback.

The message had sat unheard for nearly twenty years.

The Unraveling Begins

Gamberg teamed up with **Sheriff Greg Hagwood**, who had grown up in Quincy and still remembered the shock that swept through the community as a teenager. Together, they reopened the Keddie case—not as a favor, but as a mission.

When they compared recovered evidence with modern DNA technology, new possibilities emerged. A piece of tape from the original bindings contained partial DNA belonging to an unknown male—not any of the victims, and not the primary suspects tested earlier.

Gamberg also uncovered a report indicating that Marty Smartt had confessed to a counselor in Reno shortly after the murders, allegedly saying he had "killed Sue and Tina." The counselor's statement had been forwarded to law enforcement in 1981 and then **lost**.

By the time those revelations surfaced, both Marty and Bo were long dead. But the implications were explosive: the killers had been within arm's reach of investigators from the beginning—and someone had ensured the truth stayed buried.

Echoes of Accountability

For the surviving Sharp children, news of the reopened case was both healing and agonizing. It proved what they had always believed—that the murders weren't random, and that the original investigation had failed them.

For the community, it reopened old wounds. People who had kept silent for decades began to talk again. Some recalled seeing suspicious cars parked near Cabin 28 that night. Others admitted that fear had kept them from speaking.

Gamberg and Hagwood vowed to keep going until they either solved the case or died trying. "It's not a whodunit anymore," Hagwood said in an interview. "It's a who-covered-it-up."

The Shadow of Keddie

By the time the twenty-first century arrived, Keddie was no longer a living town but a ghost of its former self. The old resort cabins stood in ruin, overgrown with ivy and pine needles. Cabin 28 was demolished in 2004, reduced to splinters and dirt.

Yet even in destruction, it refused silence. Each new discovery— each lost file found, each DNA test processed—whispered the same truth: **this case was never cold by accident.**

Someone had buried it.

Someone had decided the Sharp family's justice wasn't worth the trouble.

And now, after decades of quiet, the walls of Keddie were beginning to speak again.

CHAPTER 7 NEW EVIDENCE, OLD WOUNDS

By the time the **Keddie murders** case reopened in the 2000s, nearly twenty-five years had passed since Cabin 28 fell silent. The pines had grown taller, the cabins older, and most of the original deputies were long retired. But in the dusty basement of the Plumas County Sheriff's Office, the ghosts of 1981 were waiting to be found.

The Box in the Basement

Investigator **Mike Gamberg** didn't expect to stumble onto the box that changed everything. He'd returned to the department after decades away, working part-time, trying to help close the old unsolved files that cluttered storage. But the Keddie case was different.

"I opened this old cardboard box," he later said, "and it was like the crime scene reached out of it. Photos, blood samples, everything we were told was lost."

Inside lay decades of negligence: fingerprint cards never processed, tape samples never tested, even an evidence envelope labeled simply *Cabin 28*. Gamberg's heart pounded as he sifted through the fragments. He had always suspected the truth had been buried—now he could prove it.

He took the case to **Sheriff Greg Hagwood**, a local who'd grown up near Keddie and still remembered the fear that swept through Quincy as a boy. Hagwood didn't hesitate.

"Let's reopen it," he said. "We owe them that."

DNA in the Tape

One of the recovered items was a length of medical tape used to bind the victims. In 1981, DNA testing didn't exist. By 2016, it did. Samples were sent to modern labs for analysis.

When the results came back, they revealed something astonishing: **the DNA of an unknown male**, not belonging to any of the victims—and not matching Martin Smartt or "Bo" Boubede, who were both long dead.

To Gamberg, this meant one thing: *there had been at least one more person inside Cabin 28 that night.*

"It told us the story wasn't finished," he said. "Whoever that third person was, he touched the bindings. He was close—close enough to feel their breath."

The discovery reignited hope. For the first time in decades, the case had scientific momentum. Yet it also deepened the mystery. If there had been three attackers, who was the third? And why had law enforcement ignored evidence pointing to multiple killers?

The Confession That Never Was

Among the rediscovered paperwork was another bombshell: a **psychologist's report** from a Veterans Administration hospital in Reno, dated 1981. The therapist wrote that his patient, *Martin Smartt*, had confessed to killing Sue Sharp and her daughter Tina. He said he'd been angry, that "Bo" had helped him, and that the police "would never pin it" on him.

The document had been sent to the Plumas County Sheriff's Office the same year—and vanished into filing cabinets for nearly four decades.

Gamberg was livid. "If that report had been acted on back then," he told reporters, "this case would've been solved within weeks."

Even more disturbing, another piece of evidence—a **taped phone call** from an anonymous man—surfaced in the same box. The caller said he had watched a news story about the discovery of Tina's remains at Feather Falls.

"I know who killed the Sharp family," the voice said.

"It was Marty Smartt and his friend, Bo."

Then the line went dead. The tape had been logged and forgotten.

Forensic analysts confirmed the recording was from the early 1980s. The voice was never identified.

Sheila's Return

When **Sheila Sharp** heard the case had been reopened, she drove back to Keddie for the first time in years. The cabins were collapsing, the woods overgrown. The spot where Cabin 28 once stood was now only an empty foundation surrounded by weeds.

"It still felt heavy there," she said quietly. "Like the air didn't move."

Gamberg met her beside the clearing. He told her about the new evidence, the DNA, the rediscovered confession. She listened without speaking, eyes fixed on the trees.

"All I ever wanted was for someone to care enough to look," she finally said.

For Sheila, the news didn't erase the trauma—but it gave it shape. The fog of mystery that had hung over her family for decades was beginning to lift.

Old Wounds, New Fire

As Gamberg and Hagwood pieced together the case, patterns emerged that made the 1981 cover-up look deliberate. Reports had been rewritten, evidence logged under wrong numbers, interviews missing.

One chilling discovery involved a **second hammer**, recovered near the crime scene years later, matching the one used in the murders. It had been found by a local in the creek behind Keddie —and turned over to police—yet no follow-up was ever done until Gamberg retested it for DNA.

Meanwhile, the sheriff's office launched a public appeal for information. Old residents began talking again. Some recalled seeing Marty and Bo burning clothes in a wood stove the morning after the murders. Others remembered Tina's frightened expression in the days before her death.

"We realized," Hagwood said, "that silence had been the killer's best friend."

The case, long buried under dust and denial, was breathing again.

What the Science Couldn't Fix

Even with modern technology, some questions refused answers. The partial DNA profile didn't match anyone in the state or federal databases. The confession letter Marty wrote to his wife was too degraded for usable prints. And Bo Boubede, rumored to have been an FBI informant, remained a ghost—his real background tangled in sealed federal files.

Still, for the first time since 1981, the Sharp family's story wasn't forgotten. The Keddie murders were no longer a cold case collecting cobwebs—they were an **open wound demanding justice.**

When asked if he believed the killers would ever be officially named, Gamberg paused.

"I already know who did it," he said. "Now I just need the proof the world can't ignore."

The Echo of Justice

Four decades after the murders, Keddie had become a ghost town. The cabins were empty, windows shattered, roofs sagging under snow. But the wind that rushed through the pines carried more than silence—it carried names.

For the Sharp children, those names meant vindication. For investigators, they meant unfinished business.

And for the forest that had once hidden so much, it meant reckoning.

The truth was finally crawling out of the dark.

CHAPTER 8 VOICES OF THE DEAD

Even after the tape recorders stopped and the crime-scene photos faded to sepia, the people of Keddie could still hear them — the voices that would not rest. They were not the whispers of ghosts in the trees, though many swore they heard those too. They were the voices of the living who had survived and those who refused to forget.

The Weight That Never Left

For **Sheila Sharp**, adulthood was a balancing act between memory and survival.

"I still wake up sometimes," she said years later, "and it's like I'm sixteen again, opening that door."

She built a life — marriage, children, even a quiet faith that steadied her — yet the past followed like a shadow that changed shape but never disappeared. Her brothers, **Rick** and **Greg**, spoke less often. Childhood trauma had stolen the language they might have used. Each handled it differently: one turned inward, the other into work and silence.

"People think time heals," Sheila once told a reporter, "but time only teaches you how to carry it without dropping it in front of everyone."

The Long Echo of Fear

For the community, the murders had cracked something spiritual.

In the years after 1981, the children who had played near the creek grew up wary, suspicious. Doors once left unlocked now clicked shut at dusk. Keddie, once a patchwork of small joys — the laughter of kids on bikes, the smell of pine sap and barbecue — turned into a place people spoke of only in past tense.

Even after the cabins emptied and the forest began reclaiming the land, visitors said the air felt wrong. Hikers reported feeling watched; others swore they heard footsteps behind them on the old logging trails.

A retired deputy said it best: *"That place doesn't make noise, it remembers."*

When the Dead Speak Through Others

Decades after the murders, journalists, podcasters, and documentary crews began arriving with cameras and questions. Some wanted to solve the crime; others wanted to sell the mystery. But for the Sharp family, every retelling was both a wound and a resurrection.

When the documentary *Cabin 28: The Keddie Murders* premiered, Sheila agreed to participate. She did it, she said, because "if people keep talking about it, maybe the truth will stay alive."

In the film, she walked through the woods where the cabin once stood, stopping at the outline of its foundation. The filmmakers caught the moment she pressed her hand against the earth. Her voice trembled: "Mom, John, Dana, Tina — I'm still here."

Those words became the heartbeat of the modern case. The victims, through memory and testimony, were still speaking.

The Investigators Who Wouldn't Let Go

Both **Mike Gamberg** and **Sheriff Greg Hagwood** knew the case might never end in a courtroom. But that didn't matter. Their purpose was to give the voiceless back their story.

Gamberg, now in his sixties, still visited the evidence room weekly, rechecking the same items, hoping technology would catch up to the fragments left behind.

"Every time I open those files," he said, "it's like they're waiting for me to finish what everyone else walked away from."

Hagwood called it unfinished business. "This case isn't about monsters in the dark," he told an interviewer. "It's about the people who ignored them."

Together they rebuilt the narrative piece by piece, knowing the killers were probably long dead — but truth, unlike flesh, doesn't decay.

The Living Legacy

In Quincy High School's library, a faded yearbook photo of Tina Sharp still sits on a shelf. Students who weren't alive when she died sometimes stop and stare at it. Teachers tell the story quietly: how a girl their age vanished, how a family was destroyed, and how justice nearly followed.

The Keddie murders became more than a crime; they became a mirror for every failure in small-town justice — the price of silence, the cost of corruption, and the resilience of the forgotten.

When asked if she still believes her mother and siblings will ever get justice, Sheila paused.

"Justice?" she repeated softly. "Maybe not the kind you can write in a report. But truth has its own way of coming home."

And in that quiet mountain valley where the trees still whisper and the air still holds its breath, the truth keeps walking — slow, patient, unstoppable.

CHAPTER 9 THEORIES THAT WON'T DIE

In every unsolved murder, the truth becomes a battlefield. Evidence turns into myth. Witnesses fade, and what's left behind —rumor, fear, fragments—grows into something larger than the crime itself.

The **Keddie murders** were no exception.

Forty years later, the case still breathes in the dark corners of the internet, in late-night documentaries, and in the minds of those who remember the silence that followed the screams. Each theory promises an answer. Each leaves something unanswered.

The Stranger Theory

In the earliest days after the murders, the sheriff's department floated a comforting idea: a stranger had done it.

A drifter, maybe. A random act. Someone passing through the

Sierra Nevada who stumbled upon Cabin 28 and unleashed unspeakable violence.

It was the theory that made Keddie sleep a little easier—because if it had been random, no neighbor needed to look at another with suspicion.

But the evidence never supported it. There was no sign of forced entry. Nothing was stolen. The attack had been up close and personal, full of rage and familiarity. Whoever did it had tied their victims carefully, spoken to them, even lingered.

This wasn't the work of a passing madman. It was someone who belonged.

Still, the stranger theory survived, whispered by those who couldn't bear to believe evil had grown roots in their own backyard.

The Insider Theory

The deeper investigators looked, the more the crime seemed to circle back toward the people of Keddie itself.

Neighbors. Friends. People who shared fences and coffee and silence.

The **Smartt connection**—Martin and his houseguest "Bo" Boubede—was the heart of this theory. Both men lived just steps away. Both were awake that night. Both lied about their alibis. And both vanished soon after.

Later discoveries—Marty's confession letter, the counselor's report, the hypnosis testimony from his own stepson—only tightened the net.

It fit too well: the jealousy, the domestic anger, the belief that Sue Sharp had urged Marilyn Smartt to leave her husband.

It explained the rage in the killings, the selective sparing of the younger children, and the removal of Tina, who may have witnessed too much.

But if the case was so clear, why had it been buried?

That question gave birth to the theory that would haunt Keddie the most.

The Cover-Up

The **cover-up theory** isn't born of imagination—it's built on what's missing.

Missing evidence. Missing reports. Missing accountability.

Sheriff **Doug Thomas's** close friendship with Marty Smartt has long fueled suspicion that the investigation was intentionally softened. Some believe higher powers intervened to protect "Bo," who was rumored to be a federal informant connected to organized crime or intelligence operations.

In that version of the story, Marty may have been a pawn—angry, unstable, used by someone who wanted the case to vanish as quickly as it erupted.

Others point to the FBI's quiet involvement after Tina's remains were found. Why had federal agents shown sudden interest in a small-town homicide that had sat cold for years? Why were so many original documents marked "restricted" or simply gone?

The deeper one digs, the murkier it becomes. But one truth remains: people in authority failed the Sharp family, whether through incompetence or intent.

The Multi-Killer Theory

When modern DNA testing revealed genetic material from an **unknown third person** on the binding tape, the puzzle twisted again. It wasn't just Marty and Bo. Someone else had been there.

Some speculate it was another local man—perhaps connected to the Smartts, perhaps tied to the region's undercurrent of drug activity. Others suggest it could have been one of the many drifters who passed through Keddie during the logging season, invited unknowingly into the wrong cabin at the wrong time.

For investigators like **Mike Gamberg**, this was confirmation of what they'd suspected all along.

"I don't think it was two men," he said. "It was three. And they weren't strangers—they were comfortable enough to stay."

The idea fits the scene's complexity: multiple bindings, multiple weapons, overlapping injuries.

But unless that third DNA sample finds a match, the theory remains an open wound.

The Internet Generation

When the case resurfaced online in the 2000s, a new wave of amateur detectives took up the torch. They dissected police files, reexamined photographs, mapped timelines, and debated motives in forums and Reddit threads.

To some, these online investigators became heroes—citizen archivists keeping the story alive. To others, they became noise, drowning the truth in speculation.

One group insisted on a link between Keddie and a string of unsolved Northern California murders, claiming a serial killer had passed through the mountains unnoticed. Another swore the case tied to a hidden drug network. A few even pushed theories involving government mind-control programs and secret military experiments.

Gamberg ignored them all.

"You can't chase ghosts," he said. "You chase what's real."

Still, the digital age gave the victims something the 1980s never did: *attention.*

Every repost, every retelling, every voice demanding answers kept their names from disappearing into history.

The Theory That Matters

When stripped of rumor and rhetoric, the Keddie murders point toward something more human than conspiracy. Not a shadowy cabal, not a drifter, but ordinary rage—jealousy, betrayal, power. A man who couldn't control his wife, a friend who shared his anger, and a system too small to handle its own darkness.

That's what makes the story unbearable. Not that it's unsolved, but that it was solvable—and wasn't.

In that truth lies the tragedy of Keddie. The killer or killers may be gone, but the silence they left behind still speaks louder than any confession.

As Sheila Sharp once said, "It's not about who swung the hammer anymore. It's about why nobody stopped them."

EPILOGUE

—The Cabin That Still Whispers

The cabin is gone now.

Cabin 28, once the scene of unspeakable violence, was demolished in 2004. The boards splintered under heavy machinery, the nails twisted loose, the floor that had held so much pain finally buried beneath the soil.

For many in Plumas County, it was an act of cleansing — the removal of a scar that had haunted them for more than twenty years. But erasing a building doesn't erase what happened inside it. The land still holds the story.

If you stand there today, just off Keddie Resort Road, the forest has almost reclaimed the space. Wild grass grows where the front steps once stood. Pine needles form a soft, uneven carpet. The breeze moves through the trees like a sigh.

And if you listen closely, the silence feels alive.

The Ghosts of the Living

For **Sheila Sharp**, that silence is both sanctuary and burden.

"I go there sometimes," she said. "Not to cry anymore, but to remember that they were real people, not a story."

Her brothers have built quieter lives. They rarely speak publicly about the murders, but each carries the invisible weight of that

April night. For them, healing isn't forgetting—it's surviving long enough to speak of it without breaking.

Sheila still advocates for victims' families, encouraging them not to give up even when the system forgets. "You never stop hoping," she says. "You just learn to live beside the hope instead of inside it."

Justice in Fragments

The **Keddie murders** remain officially unsolved, but not unspoken.

Modern DNA tests continue to probe the evidence. Files are being digitized. Every few years, the case stirs again when a new generation of journalists discovers it.

Investigator **Mike Gamberg** still keeps the box of evidence within reach. "Every item has a voice," he says. "You just have to wait for science to learn how to hear it."

Sheriff **Greg Hagwood**, before retiring, made sure the case would remain active. He called it a debt that could never be repaid but should never be ignored. "We can't promise closure," he told the press, "but we can promise truth."

Those who worked the case now measure justice in smaller victories—the rediscovered report, the verified letter, the DNA strand that may someday match a name.

The Story That Refused to Die

For decades, Keddie's tragedy has been retold in articles, documentaries, and message boards. Some come to solve it, others to feel close to the mystery. But for those who lived it, the attention is double-edged: validation wrapped in pain.

Every time someone types "Keddie murders," they resurrect a mother named **Sue**, a boy named **John**, his friend **Dana**, and a little girl named **Tina**.

The world knows their names because they never stopped whispering.

Their story endures because ordinary people—Sheila, Gamberg, Hagwood, and countless others—refused to let it fade into another unsolved file. They carried it through disbelief, bureaucracy, and time.

And that persistence became its own form of justice.

The Whisper in the Pines

When night falls over the Plumas forest, the pines sway like they're keeping secrets. Locals say you can still hear the wind hum against the empty space where the cabin once stood. Not a haunting, but a reminder.

A reminder that truth doesn't disappear when people look away.

A reminder that evil can wear familiar faces.

A reminder that silence protects no one.

Forty years have passed, and still the cabin whispers. Not of horror, but of endurance — of voices that will never go quiet until someone finally listens.

And maybe, somewhere deep in the hush of those California mountains, that's exactly what justice sounds like.

A PERSONAL REQUEST

Thank you for reading *Beneath the Pines of Keddie: Cabin 28, a Missing Girl, and the Case That Wouldn't Stay Quiet.*

If this story stayed with you—if it angered you, saddened you, or made you look twice at how silence can protect the wrong people —I would be deeply grateful if you left a review.

Even a simple star rating helps more than most readers realize. It signals to bookstores and platforms that this case still matters— and that the names at the center of it deserve to be remembered.

If you'd like to leave a review, you can visit the Amazon page here:

Or scan the QR code below to go directly to the review page:

Your support helps keep Sue Sharp, John Sharp, Tina Sharp, and Dana Wingate from being reduced to a headline—and it helps ensure stories like theirs are not quietly buried.

With gratitude,

Linda Davidson

ALSO BY LINDA DAVIDSON

CASE TIMELINE

Condensed timeline for reader orientation — expanded detail appears within chapters)

1980

- **Fall 1980** — **Sue Sharp** relocates with her children to **Keddie, California**, renting **Cabin 28** as a low-cost fresh start.

April 1981 — The Weekend Everything Changed

- **April 11, 1981 (Evening)** — Normal weekend activity in the resort community: neighbor kids move between cabins; a sleepover is planned; **Justin Smartt** stays at **Cabin 28**.
- **Late night / early hours (April 11–12)** — The attack occurs inside **Cabin 28**.
- **April 12, 1981 (Morning)** — **Sheila Sharp** returns home and discovers the scene; authorities respond.
- **Sue Sharp**, **John Sharp**, and **Dana Wingate** are found murdered.
- **Tina Sharp** is missing.
- **Rick Sharp**, **Greg Sharp**, and **Justin Smartt** are found alive in a back bedroom.

1981–1983 — The Search, the Fear, the Stalling

- **Spring–Summer 1981** — Search efforts for **Tina Sharp** expand; tips and rumors multiply; the investigation becomes plagued by confusion, contamination concerns, and community pressure.

- **1981 onward** — **Marty Smartt** and **Bo Boubede** emerge repeatedly in public discourse and later investigative arguments; both leave the area in the broader aftermath.

1984 — The Missing Girl Is Found

- **April 1984** — Human remains are discovered near **Feather Falls**; the remains are identified as **Tina Sharp**.
- The case re-enters public attention briefly, then recedes again.

2004 — The Physical Site Disappears

- **2004** — **Cabin 28** is demolished. The location remains a point of memory and controversy despite the structure's removal.

2010s — Re-Examination Era

- **2010s (Reopened momentum)** — Renewed focus on the case: previously overlooked materials are revisited, and **modern forensic testing** enters the narrative.
- **Mid-to-late 2010s** — New testing and reanalysis are discussed publicly; the case's legacy expands through documentaries, online communities, and investigative revisits.

DRAMATIS PERSONAE

(Non-spoiler overview — names and roles as used in this book)

The Sharp Family

- **Glenna "Sue" Sharp** — Single mother; moved her family to Keddie seeking a fresh start.
- **John Sharp** — Sue's eldest son; a teenager navigating small-town life and responsibility.
- **Sheila Sharp** — Sue's eldest daughter; a teenager who becomes the first discoverer of the crime.
- **Tina Sharp** — Sue's daughter; 12 years old at the time; missing after the murders.
- **Rick Sharp** — Sue's son; one of the younger children in the home that night.
- **Greg Sharp** — Sue's youngest son; asleep in the back bedroom during the attack.

The Victim from Outside the Family

- **Dana Wingate** — John Sharp's friend; present in Cabin 28 the night of the murders.

The Neighbor Child

- **Justin Smartt** — Neighborhood friend; sleeping over in Cabin 28 that night; later gives accounts that become central to theory and debate.

The Neighbors Closest to Cabin 28

- **The Seabolt Family** — Neighbors in the resort community; connected to the sleepover and the morning discovery.

Primary Persons of Interest in the Narrative

- **Martin "Marty" Smartt** — Local resident; stepfather

of Justin; appears early in the investigation and later theories.

- **John "Bo" Boubede** — Associate of Marty Smartt; frequently cited in later reporting and renewed investigation discussions.

- **Sheriff Doug Thomas** — Plumas County Sheriff during the original investigation era; leadership decisions become a major part of the book's scrutiny.
- **Investigator Mike Gamberg** — Investigator associated with later re-examination and the "rediscovered evidence" era.
- **Sheriff Greg Hagwood** — Sheriff linked to modern efforts and renewed public attention.

- **Plumas County Sheriff's Office deputies and first responders** — Initial response and early scene handling.
- **Search volunteers and community members** — Early search efforts for Tina and community fallout.
- **Forensic personnel / labs (by function)** — DNA testing, evidence handling, and re-testing later in the case.

AUTHOR'S NOTE

While every effort has been made to ensure accuracy, portions of this book rely on public records, witness accounts, and secondary reporting. Certain dialogues and private moments have been reconstructed based on verified information to reflect emotional truth and context. The intent is never sensationalism—but remembrance.

If you or someone you know has information related to the Keddie case, contact the **Plumas County Sheriff's Office** or submit a tip through official cold case channels.

Because every story deserves its ending.

SOURCES & REFERENCES

California Department of Justice. (n.d.). *Cold case files and related public records* [Agency records collection]. State of California.

Federal Bureau of Investigation. (n.d.). *Case summaries and interagency correspondence related to the Keddie murders* [FOIA-released records]. U.S. Department of Justice.

Feather River Bulletin. (1981–1984). *News coverage of the Keddie murders and related developments* [Newspaper archive]. Feather Publishing Co.

Gamberg, M., & Hagwood, G. (n.d.). *Public statements, interviews, and commentary on the Keddie homicide investigation* [Interviews].

Investigation Discovery. (2016). *Cabin 28: The Keddie murders* [Television episode]. In *People Magazine Investigates*. Investigation Discovery.

Keddie28.com. (n.d.). *Keddie murders (Cabin 28) archive: Timelines, case summaries, and compiled documents*. Retrieved Month Day, Year, from https://keddie28.com/

ABOUT THE AUTHOR

Linda Davidson is a true crime author who writes for readers who want more than shock value — they want truth with a heartbeat.

She focuses on the kinds of stories that stay with you long after the news cameras leave: unsolved murders, missing persons, rural disappearances, and investigations that never received clear answers. Instead of chasing sensational headlines, Linda writes with one question in mind: *How can I honor the victim and still tell the full truth of what happened?*

In each book, she blends careful research, clear timelines, and compassionate storytelling. Readers are guided through evidence, leads, theories, and dead ends in a way that is easy to follow and emotionally grounded. Her work keeps the victim at the center of the narrative while also examining the failures, gaps, and human decisions that shaped each case.

Linda's books are written for true crime readers who care about people, not just plot twists. She writes for those who feel frustrated by shallow coverage and are hungry for deeper, more thoughtful explorations of the cases that haunt them.

Her promise is simple:

She will research carefully.

She will explain clearly.

She will tell the truth with respect.

She will never forget that the people she writes about were real.

Linda Davidson is a true crime author dedicated to telling the stories others forget. She writes about unsolved murders, mysterious disappearances, and cold cases with a focus on the victims, their families, and the communities left behind. Combining deep research with compassionate storytelling, she helps readers make sense of complex investigations without losing sight of the human beings at the center of every case.

DISCLAIMER

This book is a work of **nonfiction** written about the 1981 Keddie murders and related developments. Every effort has been made to present the case with **accuracy, fairness, and respect for the victims and their loved ones**, using publicly available sources and widely reported records.

Because this case involves unresolved questions, conflicting accounts, and an investigation that spans decades, some details in the public record may be **incomplete, disputed, or subject to change** as new information emerges. Where sources differ, the narrative reflects that uncertainty and avoids presenting speculation as established fact.

Presumption of Innocence:

Any individuals mentioned in connection with theories, allegations, or investigative interest are **presumed innocent unless and until proven guilty in a court of law**. The inclusion of a person's name does not constitute an accusation of guilt. This book does not claim to solve the case, and no statements herein should be interpreted as legal conclusions.

Reconstructed Scenes and Dialogue:

For readability and emotional clarity, certain scenes may be **reconstructed** based on verified timelines, witness statements, and contemporaneous reporting. Any dialogue attributed to individuals is either drawn from quoted material in public sources or **recreated in a limited, reasonable way** to reflect what is known about events and context. These reconstructions are intended to convey the human reality of the case—not to sensationalize it.

Names and Privacy:

Unless a person is a clearly identified public figure or is named in widely available public records, **some identifying details may be altered** to protect privacy, particularly for private individuals who are not central to the public record.

Content Advisory:

This book contains descriptions and discussion of **homicide, violence, and the death children.** Reader discretion is advised.

No Legal or Professional Advice:

Nothing in this book is intended as legal, medical, or professional advice. Readers should consult primary documents and qualified professionals for official guidance or interpretation.

If You Have Information:

If you believe you have credible information related to this case, please contact the appropriate law enforcement agency through official channels.

— **Linda Davidson**

END NOTE

— Light in the Dark

Stories like this one walk us through some of the darkest places a human heart can go. It is easy to believe that evil has the last word—that violence, corruption, or indifference are stronger than anything else.

The Bible says something different. It tells us that God sees every unseen hurt, hears every unheard prayer, and judges every hidden deed. It also says that no life is beyond His reach, and no story is too broken to be redeemed. Justice matters to God. So does mercy. So does you.

If what you've read has stirred fear, anger, or regret in your own heart, know this: the door back to Him is never closed. Repentance is simply turning around and letting Him meet you where you are.

"Do not be overcome by evil, but overcome evil with good."

— Romans 12:21

"The light shines in the darkness, and the darkness has not overcome it."

— John 1:5

May these pages not only expose what went wrong, but also awaken a hunger for what is right—for justice, for truth, and for the kind of grace that can still save a soul.

ACKNOWLEDGMENTS

This book was written in remembrance of **Glenna "Sue" Sharp, John Sharp, Tina Sharp, and Dana Wingate**—four lives taken with a brutality that still feels impossible to hold in the mind. They were not headlines. They were not a "case." They were a mother, a son, a daughter, and a friend—people with routines, dreams, small joys, and ordinary moments that mattered. May their names be spoken with care, and may their memory outlive the silence that followed.

I also want to acknowledge the **surviving family members** and loved ones who have carried the weight of this tragedy for decades. Grief does not end when the cameras leave, when the tapes stop recording, or when the public's attention shifts. It becomes something you learn to live beside. If any pages in this book hold tenderness, it is because the story demands it—because the cost of this crime was not only measured in lives lost, but in lives altered forever.

My deepest gratitude goes to the **journalists, investigators, archivists, and independent researchers** who refused to let this story disappear into a forgotten file cabinet. Without persistent reporting, careful recordkeeping, and the patient assembling of timelines, the Keddie case would be even more obscured than it already is. Thank you to those who documented what could be documented, asked questions when answers were inconvenient, and preserved fragments that time—or institutions—might otherwise have erased.

I am also grateful to the **law enforcement professionals** who, across different eras, continued to revisit this case when it would have been easier to let it remain buried. Cold cases survive on endurance: the willingness to re-check what others dismissed, to re-test what technology once couldn't read, to listen again to the voices that were ignored the first time. Whatever conclusions history ultimately reaches, the act of continuing to look matters—because it affirms that the victims mattered.

To the wider community of people who keep victims' stories present—through documentaries, long-form reporting, responsible forums, and public awareness—thank you for remembering with seriousness. True crime can easily drift toward spectacle. This case requires the opposite: restraint, accuracy, and respect. It requires a commitment to truth without turning suffering into entertainment. When the conversation stays human, memory becomes a form of protection.

Finally, to my readers—true crime enthusiasts, justice seekers, and quiet witnesses who turn these pages with heavy attention—thank you. Your compassion is the difference between consumption and care. You are the reason these stories remain more than mystery. You are the reason names don't vanish. And if this book leaves you with one lasting feeling, I hope it is this: **that truth is not only something we find—it is something we choose to keep alive.**

— **Linda Davidson**

Printed in Dunstable, United Kingdom